THE BLACK BEAR INSIDE ME

Pitt Poetry Series

Ed Ochester, Editor

THE BLACK BEAR INSIDE ME

ROBIN BECKER

University of Pittsburgh Press

Published by the University of Pittsburgh Press, Pittsburgh, Pa., 15260
Manufactured in the United States of America
Printed on acid-free paper
10 9 8 7 6 5 4 3 2 1

ISBN 13: 978-0-8229-6524-4
ISBN 10: 0-8229-6524-0

Cover art: Woman and Bear, a paper cut by Harriet M. Rosenberg
Cover design by Melissa Dias-Mandoly

In memory of Maxine Kumin, 1925–2014
and Victor Kumin, 1921–2016

CONTENTS

I

II

III

THE BLACK BEAR INSIDE ME

I

Clearing

Since Harvey's on his tractor for the first
cutting of the summer I'm glad I picked
paintbrush hawkweed and daisies early
this morning   Wild turkeys squawking at the edge
of the mowing complain his noisy occupation
displeases them exposed to fox and falcon now
Where will they hide to feed   He chose today
for the dry breeze rifling rush and bluestem

All of July and August lie ahead but I want only June
light dappling mountain ash   They say to live in the present
requires we let go every second of our lives
He keeps a mowing by mowing for July's meadow rue
and asters   To live in the present they say become a fern
a prism a membrane through which time mows

Moment of Amazement

As if to linger, unhurried, in the quiet
afterlude of her arrival, the unnamed

newborn in my cousin's arms unfurled
long fingers and stretched open her mouth

which issued a simple, oblong yawn.
With undulating hands, she sieved the new

nothing of air, all dark hair and lashes,
a creature so slick she seemed to be still

breathing underwater on feathery gills.
Of her mother's skin and smell she partook

already; also of her father's, holding
her two year-old sister near, so she could

see and touch the journey on the creature.
Close by, the midwife in her scrubs

wrote notes, then leaned in towards the family
of four, that, moments ago, had been three.

I left before the living wail shattered
the hum of monitors and murmurs, but

in the relief and exhaustion of that room
I saw the mouth find the breast and latch on.

Two Dogs, One Wise

The gentle purebred bought
at eight weeks lies down

beside his bowl and looks away
towards the mountain, permitting
the damaged dog to lick his bowl

He has the wisdom of one well-loved
from birth who learned to ignore the growls
and lunges of the dog who lost

her place and was sent away
and whom I rescued   He turns his gaze from her
as the books explain a superior dog

will do to avoid a confrontation
She circles his bowl, she stands between him
and his bowl but he is listening

with his nose and his tail to a distant
music the beloved carry inside them

Elegy for the Science Teacher

Maria D. Peters, 1915–2013

Mrs. Peters has died at 98 and I'll never get a chance
to apologize for all the trouble I brought to 7th grade
science, where she demonstrated how the folding-door
spider dug ten-inch tunnels into rotting logs with
spiny mandibles and lined the walls with silk
and left a bit hanging out to form a door from which
it catapulted after dark. In the circus of natural history
I was the class clown, she the vivarium; her faith included

the decomposing log and the chemical chatter of beetles.
Born in Breslau in 1915 she spoke with a German accent
about *British Soldiers*—the red-capped lichen that thrives
on decaying conifer—and the slimy slug that propels itself
with an undulating muscular foot along the forest floor.
Colonies of carpenter ants and bees proved the Quaker
principle of cooperation: her ecosystem, her religion. In London
during the war, she taught Basque refugees by speaking Latin.

I failed to plot the simple graph on Darwinian snails.
She pioneered the PA School of Horticulture for Women
where girls kept bees, canned fruit, learned farm carpentry
and soil science, studying the energetic sow bug with seven pairs
of legs and a carapace of overlapping plates. Recently, people
have come around to her belief in conservation, sustainability.
A tiny woman, sometimes for emphasis she would pull
out the bottom drawer of her desk and stand on it. We all laughed.

Ah, Mrs. Peters, did the inter-relatedness of fungal spore and wind
move you to drive the Schuykill Expressway every Tuesday
to pack up clothes for needy families? I could not appreciate
the watershed you made of your life, linking all living
things by a common course. Twenty years ago, at a reception
you told me of your father's best friend, a Jewish scientist who
refused to leave Germany in 1935. *My father begged him to go*
you said. *My father cried* you said. *He never forgot him.*

Bluefish, 1970

My first summer in P-town neighbors taught me *Putanesca*
oil capers olives marinating fish in the tiny kitchen
of the 3-bay half- cottage I rented with my unemployment
check blocks off Commercial Street
where the drag queens called *Hello, Dolly*
and bluefish sold for $3.99 lb all summer

At Race Point fisherman anchored in wet sand fought
the indigo wind the inky surf bluefish on their lines and
in coolers and in the A & P where I stared at the handsome
butch women with their girlfriends in town for a week
from Kansas and Ohio desire thrumming the narrow
streets and the clamorous angles of Provincetown's

rooftops desire incoming as the tide I read and wrote
by day and thereby earned my nightly trip to the women's bar
to disco to cigarettes and the compulsive disappointment of leaving
alone at 2 a.m. for home past revelers sharing pizza at *Spiritus*
you never know what the senses will retain just last week
at the market I overheard *look they have bluefish today*

Coppice and Pollard

1

When I asked Harvey what to do
        about the wicker porch chair

with the broken reeds,
        he said that since the woven strands

had not received a coat of paint,

        I could just throw it
in the woods. He said the local barns

        are filled with just
such chairs that someone swears

        he'll fix someday. A neighbor

used to keep a coppice stand; she sold
        to crafters, by the foot,

the hazel and willow she tended— by cutting
        plants back to the ground.

She said a hazel tree could live a thousand years

        if coppiced properly.
From her stand, they made fencing,

        tool handles and chairs
like mine, whose narrow arms and modest back

        suggest a woman's frame.

2

In Amsterdam, pollarded plane trees gave
        the boulevards a brutal look,

the thick trunks capped with whorls
        of angry fists. In college then,

I knew nothing of harvesting wood
        without killing the tree,
or feeding goats on a fodder of leaves and twigs—

        cut from rows of lindens trimmed
to free the air for windmills in Dutch towns,

        a point of civic pride: well- tended trees.

3

        Though Harvey thinks
I'll throw it out of sight, I set the chair

        at woods edge,
a natural throne repurposed for the birds.

        A standing dead
snag and basal scars on the red oak

by the neglected stone wall—
        all signs. I've learned to read

        the history of these fire-adapted
hardwoods and white pines,

        where hunters once
burned the understory to the ground

to move without
a sound and sight small game,

before Harvey's grandfather
built these camps by hand

and down the road,
a woman kept a coppiced wood.

Yankee Barn Sale

For Frankie B. Tolman

The handsome frockcoat didn't button but I fell in love
with the toy rocking horse, red paint peeling, real

horsehair on mane and tail which the vendor said belonged
to her grandmother, she couldn't keep everything,

including the double blue-and-white striped stoneware
mixing bowls and free-standing beveled mirror

now detached from its tiger oak dresser. Easy to love
the world at 7:30 a.m., Harvey hauling to his truck

the talismanic, reconditioned arc welder
from the small appliance section and our neighbor

Martha hailing us to model her flea market barn
jacket and tartan vest. On that appointed, breezy Saturday

in July, as under a bell-shaped dome, our fancies took
form, seduced by vintage doll houses patinaed with the play

of tiny hands, woven leather snow shoes and *Shakespeare*
casting reels in their original boxes. Like the iron doorstop,

Time waited for me to admire her weight and finish:
a marbled, green inkwell cocooned in velvet;

a porcelain, enameled gasoline sign; a 1930s,
crystal, lemon juicer, its history in my palm.

Ravished by objects, for a $1.00 parking fee,
I was transported to Edinburgh, 1819, where Marty

paraded in jabot and brooch and Old Sutherland kilt.
I strolled into the Gilded Age, as Frankie walked past

toting an antique cast iron and glass terrarium— miniature,
Victorian conservatory—in which a tiny chamber

group rehearsed a late Beethoven string quartet,
ferns rising around them in a 19th century heaven.

Reading Music

When the twenty-five-year-old violin
teacher in tank top and shorts moves my first
finger to D *in third position on*
the A string I understand why I could

not reproduce the tune as I heard it
Bach chose B flat and E flat
for this minuet in Suzuki Book III
The four notes rise and cascade down

ring in the slightly mournful pitch I love
to produce and do now and will over
and over to practice this sliding

of the hand up to third position I can't
describe the music but I can describe
the taste of getting it right

of downshifting to first before the run
of seven notes up from D to C oh
I remember when at five the marks on
the page became a story

Scottish Melodies

When they play the strathspey
Marshall wrote for Mrs. Gordon of Park,
the fiddler remembers the mowing
meadow once on common land,
and when they play "Marquis of Huntley's Farewell"
the pianist knows the son must leave his home,

and the open field system
must give way to enclosure and lament.
To the "Mortlach Reel" and
"Anderson's Rant" we will dance
in the hills of displacement
and in the town hall of good manners

where the youngest learns to keep
her weight on the outside foot
and circle right. Of the history
of northeast Scotland, we have 262 tunes
that may be played at different speeds
whether for dancing or listening

to the tragedy of the commons,
in matters of resources like air and water
which must be taught to every generation—
like learning to spot by keeping your eyes
on your partner's eyes when dancing,
so as not to get dizzy and spin

down the middle without your feet.
To the tunes of William Marshall,
played in Nelson, New Hampshire, the caller
will ask all dancers to bow to their neighbors,
a practice the Highlanders carried with them
from the Clearances to Cape Breton and Cape Fear.

Hearing the News

In memory of Max

I call the dog and walk
    down the mowing
        wondering how dying

dares to haunt
    this breezy summer day.
        An old question

you'd reply and mention
    Auden, his way
        with boys falling from skies.

You'd hoist a hay bale
    with one strong arm—wisps sailed
        among the flies—

then plunge your scoop
    into the bin. Loose grain
        clattered like rain.

I loved to watch you move
    around the barn.
        Tan, in a sleeveless shirt,

you cinched the girth
    on a bay horse. The farm
        bustled with guests

who wanted to be close
    and you played host
        to all. How blessed

to follow you
    uphill and skinny dip
        where stocked trout flipped . . .

Summer ripened the new
        pole beans and peas.
                From trees marked for thinning

wafted spinning
        red ribbons. Did it ease
            your agnostic

perspective (Jewish soul?)
        to see bodies of whole
            beloved horses lifted

into graves you pondered
        from your windows?
            I move with

heavy wonder
        at your slowing. You'd groan
            snap out of it,

then go upstairs to pick
        on your poems,
            your *bone pile.*

Whitetail Spring

To keep the newborn free of scent a doe
(I almost stepped, I thought at first, on a fox)

will consume her fawn's urine and droppings
and abandon a newborn camouflaged

motionless in the dappled grass
if she detects a human scent.

The fawn looked at me, aroused,
inquisitive, not yet imprinted on her mother.

They will sometimes follow any larger creature,
a person for example. I wanted to touch her

fearless silky side while her mother fed
somewhere nearby, the sun-flecked afternoon

grown dangerous with human desire.

The Black Bear Inside Me

All summer I elude them—
who think they want to see

my three cubs someone
said she spotted

on the gravel road that severs
thick woods

near a row of mailboxes,
by the stream;

who take the path down
and up the mowing

with baskets on their arms,
fearful

when they hear me
huff or blow.

They know
I will outrun, outswim,

out-climb, bluff-charge,
and in winter

drop my heart rate
from 40 to 8 beats a minute

in my den of
wind-thrown trees.

They know they will take
me in the September

kill, harvesting
my kind with dogs

and guns, and they know
we haven't taken one of them

since 1784 in this state
where 5,000 black bear

clear carcasses
of deer and moose

and sow
fruit trees and shrubs.

They know they need us
who are so like them

our numbers tell
the story, yes, the land

that supports us
supports them; without us,

adapted to scarcity and woodland
loss, they're going down.

Theory

As the animal returns on a beaten path
to the den, we go back over the facts
certain we ignored clear signs.

I left for Italy that summer, though
she had quit her job and moved back home.
I knew it signaled a bad turn but chose

the Tuscan love affair in the seventeenth-century
olive mill. We say we *survive* our siblings'
suicides, meaning we stood with our parents

at the unthinkable graves. In one theory,
the troubled family sacrifices one member,
as plants surrender leaves in times of drought.

Alex, an Obituary

His name stood for Avian Learning Experiment.

She bought him in a pet shop. He learned to identify

six shapes and five colors. Correcting Griffin, the younger

bird, he shouted, *Six not four!* Had to endure hundreds of

repetitions to achieve statistical importance. He would

say *want to go back* and she would say *have a nut.*

He would say *want a banana, want a carrot,*

and she would say *you're just interrupting our work.*

At thirty, he had the emotional life of a two-year old

human child. Each night, when she put him back

in his cage, he said *I love you. See you tomorrow.*

Hummingbird

I love the whir of the creature come
to visit the pink
flowers in the hanging basket as she does

most August mornings, hours away
from starvation to store
enough energy to survive overnight.

The Aztecs saw the refraction
of incident light on wings
as resurrection of fallen warriors.

In autumn, when daylight decreases
they double their body weight to survive
the flight across the Gulf of Mexico.

On next-to-nothing my mother
flew for 85 years; after her death
she hovered, a bird of bones and air.

The Collection of the Canter

Three days a week, into that stable of pre-adolescence
I strode, where the smell of *Absorbine*
and hoof dressing rose astringent from the cross ties,
where a girl in muddy boots circled a curry comb,
where the language of bridles and bits rolled in my mouth
as I said *D-Ring Snaffle* and *Rubber Pelham,*
Kimberwicke and *Hackamore.* And I learned

a horse must come to the bit, you cannot force
him to collect himself, you must ask him
with your weight and legs and hands. The girl
walked her horse into his stall, unbuckled the halter,
and hugged the V where the breastplate left
a sweaty place she scrubbed away.

We grazed them on braided nylon ropes or leather
lead shanks. Tornado, the open jumper, wore quilted leg wraps
daredevil Debbie knelt to secure. Summer
Saturdays we trailered to shows, entered *classes*
where I came to understand *class* as *the father who rises*
at five to pack hoof pick and shedding blade. My father
didn't see the point, came late, wore white loafers. I was

the only Jew until Judy Cohen came with her black
thoroughbred, her father, the rabbi, known to my family.
Throatlatch, cavesson, browband, laced rein. I loved
the bridle's vocabulary, the music of *martingale* and *curb chain*
hanging in the tack room, where I came to understand *class*
as Stubben saddles with brass name plates. I never

had the confidence but I had an ear. I never liked
the nervous circling before the jumps or jumping
but I loved the words *oxer, wing standards, jump cup,*
women in show coats and proper fawn breeches, gloved hands
steady at the withers, at the sitting trot, at the collected
canter, over the jumps and then the slow circle to mark
a faultless round, applause, doff of the hat.

She swung her leg over and casually slid off,
reins in one hand, a Coke someone gave her in the other,
glamorous even in the exercise paddock, counting off strides
between jumps. You never lose your early memory of class: tack room
with gleaming bridles hanging in a figure-8 style, where
you waited, belonging, with the others for your ride home.

True Blue Communications Man

He called the company *No Clue* said he
was *getting out and getting into aquaculture*
he'd worked in cable eighteen years and swapping
out my modem said *instead of upgrading lines*
Verizon sold to True Blue cutting half the road crew

Look he said taking out his iphone *I grow basil*
broccoli carrots peppers strawberries anything
you want in water full of nitrates put out by my tilapia
it's a beautiful system he said *entirely*
self-contained all elements recirculating

How could I tell him I had to get back to work
as he flashed photographs of cauliflower
generously shaped and fanning from grow-buckets

My old man used to work for the post office
then they started taking away his route
street by street cutting down his hours he had
nothing to spend in the neighborhood back
when money used to circulate in the community

Who would think fish poop and pee could nourish
a garden to perfect chemical balance I see
hydroponics as a model for the future a sustainable
medium it's visionary like new societies using solar
panels and alternative energy no limits

How great his need to speak I looked at my watch
he didn't notice from the window I could see his truck
his eighteen years of cable and test machinery

This is a small town but corporations have taken
out feed and shoe stores appliance stores I'm trying
to set an example for my sons, the little one eats sprouts
by the handful, the 12 year-old helped me install
the pump that kicks on when it hits a set point and

automatically raises or drains the water
that soaks the roots of the plants I love
the symbiosis between fish and vegetables
we freeze can and preserve and still have more
than we can use I was all set to open up a shop

everything you need for backyard hydroponics
garden towers grow-buckets aqua-pond pumps
but I couldn't get a small business loan
although the location was perfect and
the banker couldn't believe my tomatoes

Missing

In memory of Charles Harmon, 1942–1973

My Russian grandmother claimed she hated
        everything Russian except
Anna Karenina and Rachmaninoff.

Against ambiguity in history
        and politics,
she insisted that good and evil were,

like beauty, apparent to everyone.
        Though I argued against
her way of thinking, I inherited it: her

disdain for the contingent; her rejection
        of uncertainty; her fidelity
to all matters already settled

by the application of clear rules
        to which all reasonable
persons adhered. Anyone could agree

that Lyndon Johnson, while not a handsome
        man, became a good
president by legislating the War on Poverty,

conceived years before by Roosevelt.
        (May his name
be for a blessing.) There was no discussing

Shostakovich whose music *pounded like*
        guns entering a village and then screeched
like terrified peasants. He took a simple

Jewish folk tune and made it crazy; what
        kind of music is that?
I left Russia to get away from those people.

And so I took an unalloyed pleasure
        in suggesting
we watch Jack Lemmon, portraying

an America businessman, searching
        for his disappeared son
in Costa-Gavras' *Missing*. I studied

my grandmother, with her needful faith
        in U. S. policy,
as she watched a helpless father—who trusts

his State Department—ask for
        and receive no help
from the U.S. embassy officials in Santiago

who, the film slowly reveals, had a hand
        in his son's murder.
It never happened, she said, narrowing her eyes

at me, *our country wouldn't do that*, she said,
        going into the kitchen,
angry with me for engineering the movie's

outcome just to bully her. And I felt ashamed
        for bullying her and afraid
of the U.S. Army School of the Americas

and of my own desperate longing: for a system
        in which I could put my faith,
profess my adherence, and get on with it.

Security Clearance

The tall one wore a grey raincoat, and the
short one in a beige raincoat said they knew
he'd been my student, they wouldn't take much
of my time, it was a government matter.
They sat in the chairs where my students sit
for conferences and took out notebooks,
like students, and then one asked, *Does he have
any reason to do harm to America?*
Once Daniel brought to seminar a poem
about Mount Namsan and the Han River,
set in Korea, where he'd gone over
Christmas break to see his mother, a lieutenant
stationed in Yongsan. I urged him to think
about grad school but he wanted Army Intelligence.
What did he like to do in his spare time?
He wrote poetry, I said. *He wrote poetry*, the
short one repeated and the tall one wrote it down,
repeating *poetry*. *How would you characterize
his temperament? Mild?* one coached.
Easily riled? The smart girl with spiky,
purple hair liked to sit beside him. The only
black student in the class, he never spoke
about race when race surfaced in seminar.
Use of drugs or alcohol? I called on him
 when we talked about craft. *Daniel*, I asked,
what do you hear in the music of these lines?
He studied all weekend, an Honors student,
a double-major. He often put his head down
on the desk, resting as the others drifted in,
as if he needed to conserve energy.
On the incarceration of black men
in our country, on the presidency
of Barack Obama, we never spoke. *Would he
have any reason to be angry
at the United States?* We looked at his line
turns, talked about syntax and diction. He read
Keats and Komunyakaa; loved choosing

odd verbs and offbeat images; knew indirection
sometimes works best—shifting pace and tone.
What can you say that would help us evaluate
Daniel's suitability for sensitive work?
The last time I saw him, he said he'd gotten
some sleep and was moving to D.C.
to await his security clearance.
You could get a fellowship to grad school,
I repeated. *You wouldn't have to pay.*
You always pay, he said and shook my hand.
Thank you for your time, the tall one said.
Is there anything you would like to add
about Daniel's character or work ethic?
Once he brought to class a poem in which
the speaker takes a gun apart and re-assembles
it after cleaning. I figured his mother
taught him how to do it: the poem
showed a loving attention to detail.

The Wages of Sin

New neighbors down the road posted a sign
that reads *The wages of sin is death. None
come to the Father but by me.* Atrocity

alters how language comes to us. *Orlando:*
American shorthand for tragedy
no Magic Kingdom can undo. *Newtown.*

Columbine. The semi-automatic slaughters
light names with a detonating charge.
He who worked for Disney's wages will return

neither to his father nor to anyone.
How to love my neighbor as myself, then?
I can't. Gay kids who went to dance at Pulse

pay with their lives, while down the road, the sign—
God's gift to us: eternal life through Christ—

Ballroom

For Suzy Colt

I didn't know a polonaise from east coast swing
  the day I said I'd come
  watch you perform
while our mutual friend lay suffering.

Your ballroom lessons included tango
  and waltz, foxtrot and
  the Latin rhythms;
you practiced— during the year of her slow

decline— *traveling back and forth in the slot,*
  the anchor step, the right
  side pass, hijacking the lead.
Concentration meant that you forgot,

for an hour, twice a week, her increased
  frailty, moodiness.
  We onlookers took seats
around the room. Beginners counted beats

as they stared into one another's eyes.
  You clapped for every
  couple on the floor,
waiting in your skin-tight femme disguise.

Was I the only one who gasped when you
  clasped your female teacher's hand
  and snapped your head?
Inches between your breasts, your bodies flew

and mesmerized, I saw the tango as
  the smooth mirroring
  of same-sex bodies.
After a break, you danced to Latin jazz

(Jill-and-Jill alongside Jack-and-Jills),
        the mambo, samba, rumba.
        Your locked-eyes intimacy
made me turn away, stunned by the skills

you mastered that sad year, when dancing
        took you to Buenos Aires,
        studying complex steps in pairs—
each learned maneuver life-enhancing.

At the Memorial

Dying she chose the farmhouse the tablecloths the flourless chocolate
cake the Prosecco the prosciutto the pink and white peonies she
arranged for us the tastes and smells she loved and one

by one in the sunny parlor we try to say what we admired
what we will miss a dog sleeps on the 19th century
floorboards pictures of her as a precocious child with her brother

today a stocky man with heavy glasses and pictures of her in college
with the beautiful black dancer she loved who died of AIDS
twenty years ago his framed portrait stood on her nightstand at the end

her best friend has to stop herself from trying to say everything
she wants to say no end to the qualities she possessed her great
intelligence her fierceness she reads One Art by Bishop and sits down

in a white wicker chair on the screened-in porch the late June
afternoon gives way and almost everyone has a life to return to

On the Grand Canal

In doublet with hanging sleeves
I dressed for the masquerade
at the palace but never arrived,
because another Venetian experience

required getting lost at night
on narrow streets and feeling a frisson
of fear and genuine, erotic danger.
For my bohemian, Peggy Guggenheim

experience, I stepped from the water taxi
into modernism, into the gift shop—
unburdening an epic
discharge of traveler's checks.

In Santa Maria della Pieta, I learned
I belonged to the Baroque—
more rotund red priest in hose
and wig at the clavichord

than trim expatriate socialite,
though I could imagine feeling
like someone whose father went
down with the Titanic.

Provisional Ode

You love a rented place, someone gone
and you employ her stoneware, her study, her stove.

Water the bougainvillea blooming
in the solar bath; shutter the great blinds

that lower temperature and light.
Like the burrowing owl, you sleep under

ground, tunneled into the mesa— and live
with the errant wind that lashes your fears.

Your mother called you crazy, which meant she
was still alive and you could set yourself

against the totem pole of her opinions.
Twenty years ago she wanted you to have

a desert home; she saw your happiness
at seven thousand feet, and you declined.

You could love the cans and tires filled with sand
by the outrider architect only

if they belonged to someone else. You wanted
a tenancy, provisional as sun on adobe walls,

and at night, the cobalt and turquoise silence,
the occasional meteor for company.

Men as Friends

I have a few which is news to me
Tom drops by in the mornings with his travel
mug my mother would call it a coffee klatch

we review our terrible histories with fathers
and talk about the father he's become and how much
it will cost to replace gutters the ice brought down

and then there's soft-spoken Harvey
with whom I enjoy long pauses in conversation about how
they raised the Nelson town hall and put a foundation underneath

during which we both look up at Mt. Monadnock and then down
at the ground and then back at each other silence precipitating
the pretty weather we share before he goes inside for lunch

when I had to pack up my office Tom boxed
and loaded books into my car I didn't think he'd want to
but his idea of friendship includes carrying heavy things

at the dog park the retired Marine with the schnauzer
asked *Do you have a husband?* I replied *I don't care for men
in that way* as a Marine James mostly played cards

on a supply ship now he mostly hunts and fishes
climbs his orchard ladder for my Cortlands
and in trout season leaves, in my fridge, two rainbows

Semblance

The dog I love is turning into my father
an old man I have to humor to get up
do his business he even growls like my father

and gives me the eye I never know what kind
of mood I'll find when he wakes from a nap
and with stiff joints makes his way to the kitchen

when it rains he turns from the door whining
peckish when it snows he refuses to wear a coat
when people visit he remembers his old

manners and sometimes joins us on the couch
and falls asleep snoring like my father who
never had much use for my conversation

and showed his teeth when I
displeased him collared as he was
and made to heel by his betters

after guests leave he stares at his food sometimes
I ignore him sometimes I plunge my hands
into the smelly stuff and he eats from my palm

The Broker

With the loupe in his eye the jeweler tapped
pearls to his teeth, clinked charms on his scale
and made piles of 14 and 18 karat,
humming, calculating his chances

of finding, through the right dealer, someone
between fifty and eighty for the heart-
shaped pendant to wear at the opera,
with wrists small enough for the gold bamboo

bracelet and matching earrings; without
access to cash, my mother understood
currency exchange and asset allocation,
knew gold could string a loan or buy a ticket

out of a marriage or travel across
kingdoms and continents, and how, each birthday,
women's money might compound in the form
of a ruby-studded locket on a braided

chain or a ring with fluted rows
of diamonds and filigree, carefully tied up
in a silk bag which I now hand over
to this agent who will negotiate the best

sale he can manage, figuring in his
twenty percent commission, a fee
I accept as I receive the empty
velvet ring tray and satin travel

organizer with the tiny pockets,
each with a tiny zipper to safeguard
the freedom my mother amassed and passed
on to me, illiquid until I zero out.

The Annual Performance Review

Though you failed to complete your Wellness Profile
and Preventive Physical Exam Certification, you did
attend a biometric screening session, for which

you participated in the Company Fast. Your Body
Mass Index placed you in the average-to-low sector
at the annual department fall picnic.

You may respond to the review though I
advise against it. Retaliation has been a persistent
problem with the system, and though technicians

are working to resolve the issues, they have not
succeeded. Your successes, however, we have
properly recorded in the Extra Large-Array Digital

Humanities Storage Facility. You may visit
the facility by logging on and teleporting
through the department coffee machine, located

in the former mailroom, currently serving
as the Center for Corporate Branding Operations.
Thank you for all you do for the department.

Taken into Account

How to account for the lacerated hands
of the enslaved, 15-year-old Cambodian deckhands

whose infections come from the gills of the fish
they sort and the nets they sew, eighteen hours a day, fishing

in *floating labor camps* the waters off Thailand
to supply the Songla Canning Public Company of Thailand?

And how to account for the bribes of the desperate trafficker—
whose own sons roam in rags the streets of Bangkok traffic—

whose promises to guide the migrant boys to decent jobs disappear
inside the shipping crate, where boys, stashed for days, are disappeared.

*. . . to get tangled in the mesh and yanked underwater, it is
likely that no one would notice right away. The work is*

frenzied and loud, as the boys chant in unison while pulling the nets.
And how does one account for the captain, who must net

more and more kidnapped migrants, as some jump overboard or die
from beatings or try to escape to other ships rather than die

in darkness, casting at night a seine net, barefoot, on the slick deck?
And what of unmoored winches and tackle, sliding across the deck

to fracture a femur or rip into a thin thigh? On the South China Sea
you belong to the captain. No laws protect you when no one can see.

The Barcelona Inside Me

Give me, again, the fairy tale grotto
with the portico-vaulting overhead.
Let me walk beneath the canted columns
of Gaudi' s rookery, spiral
along his crenelated Jerusalem
of broken tiles, crazy shields.
Yes, it's hot as hell and full
of tourists at the double helix,
but the anarchists now occupy
the Food Court, and the Arcadian dream
for the working class includes this shady
colonnade cut into the mountainside.
I've postponed my allegiance to
the tiny house movement, to the 450
square feet of simple, American maple
infrastructure and the roomy
mind suspended like a hammock
between joists. Serpents and castle
keeps shimmer, and a mosaic invitation
to the Confectionery gets me a free
café con leche on *La Rambla,*
where honeycombed apartments bend
on chiseled stone and host
floating, wrought-iron balconies.
I think I'll move into Gaudi's dream
of recycled mesh, walk barefoot
on his flagstone tiles
inscribed with seaweed
and sacred graffiti
from pagan tombs.
0, Barcelona of chamfered corners!
And chimneys of cowled
warriors! From Gaudi's Book
of Revelations, I invite the goblet
and the stone Mobius strip
to a *tapas* of grilled prawns and squid.

Rodeo Ben

1893–1985

Happy Trails to you, Bernard Lichtenstein,
Tailor to the Stars, who outfitted Gene Autry
and Roy Rodgers and little riders like me
at 6240 North Broad Street and Godfrey,
across from the Hot Shoppe,

where, in 1959, my father ordered the mouth-
numbing *orange freeze*. We watched
the door for bronco busters coming in for lunch,
and once he swore he saw Hopalong Cassidy
get into a Cadillac. Bernie, you recast the man

from Lodz—immigrant stitcher for *Blue Bell*
and *Wrangler*—as *Rodeo Ben*, the Yiddish-speaking
King of Cowboy Wear. From Cincinnati, Leonard
Franklin Slye emerged a singing buckaroo;
Lucille Wood Smith fashioned herself into

the wholesome Dale Evans, riding *Buttermilk*,
envy of young cowgirls who copied her
style at *Rodeo Ben's* in fringed vests and
turquoise shirts embroidered with cactus flowers.
I wanted tan breeches and a black

melton jacket, a velveteen-covered helmet
and tall leather boots. Ben sold those, too.
For "English" riders, out came ratcatcher and stock
pin with a tiny horse's head encased in acrylic.
"Don't Fence Me In" played in the background

as I tried to look like Althea Roger-Smith, British
show-jumper and winner of the Queen Elizabeth Cup.
My father pulled out his wallet, I gathered up my boxes,
dreaming myself into a tale of pluck,
no longer that terrified girl at the post-and-rail

who couldn't get her timing right and rose
seconds late from the saddle and who, when her horse
veered from the fence, corkscrewed headfirst into it.
I never left that frightened girl behind
in the dressing room at *Rodeo Ben's,*

though I tried. Each time I saw the ambulance
parked by the show ring, I knew it waited for me,
and for my father, climbing in beside me, fumbling
with the buttons on the expensive shirt, as the siren
rang out our sweet, unsustainable dreams.

Make It Plain

In memory of Miriam Goodman, 1939–2008

At August's end I make a last bouquet—
the asters (white and purple), goldenrod,
a nodding thistle, baneberry, hawkweed.

I use my friend's old *Field Guide*; in the book,
her twenty-year-old chart of flowers glimpsed
for two decades from June to fall's first freeze.

Dear Miriam, your handwritten life list
betrays you as a lover of the world
and of the words that make it plain to us

though documents, like directions, can confound
when someone says *turn left where the ochre
house used to sit* or *seen off Chesham Road.*

You suffered all the usual assaults,
the body's failures, friendships gone adrift.
Maybe that's why I like to think of you

pulling off the road in mid-July
to jot down *sundew, pitcher plant, toadflax,*
and *strange pink cluster near Leadmine Quarry.*

This search to match a flower to its name
can lend a certain order to the day
as well as give a shape to solitude,

yours, mine. Brave, like you, a little lonely
my bouquet on your table stands.

Where the Unfairness of the World Resides

Into his bolstered bed, he withdraws,
a nautilus closing
up shop with a leathery hood. *Who*

rescued whom? the bumper sticker asks
five days after
the massacre in Orlando, where, six

states away, I drive him to the vet
who confirms he's going
blind and deaf. Oh, parchment-colored dog,

your fearful growl at my approach reveals
the original cruelties
we could never erase but held at bay

for years—like papyrus tightly scrolled.
Derangement
of your senses and mistrust beset you,

leave me to leave you alone, delicate
paws shielding the face
where the unfairness of the world resides.

Blast Off

I'm ready for the next phase, the one
in which the only daily obligations:
reading Vasko Popa's *Collected*,

hand weights after the treadmill,
and practicing Bach gavottes on violin.
Still, I know the next phase will bring

its own *tsuris*—incremental
joint failure, tsunamis of loss.
Like everybody, I'm loathe to trade

the indenture I know for woe
I can only imagine. Saying *I'm ready*
isn't exactly true; it's practicing.

Words with Friends

Though not a competitive person, I do
like to give my friends good game and so
I've spent the better part of a morning

studying "legal" words with the letter *K*
and found that great chunks of social history
may reside in a single letter when applied

to the cultural geography of food. Without
an official *okeh* (11 points) I can't make *kofta*
(ground lamb with parsley, garlic and lemon)

or *kidreh*—a dish that would surely bring
to the table Palestinian and Israeli to debate
the arrangement of rice and lamb in the pot

and thereby pave the way for a sustainable
peace, much as the legal *kibbeh* (17 points)
links Arabic and Sephardic cuisine

with allspice and pine nuts rolled between hands.
Imagine Jerusalem united over *kuku* (illegal),
everyone waiting to add yogurt and cucumber

to the frittata of baked fava beans
and bayberries, eggs cooked just right.

The Fix

Harvey says *it'll hold for now* meaning the gasket
he's rigged to stop the leak in the water tank

it's what he says when he conjures a grasp of wood
notched to catch a door that always swung shut his supply

of couplers and pipe makes visible the makeshift
nature of our daily operations the contingencies

he concocts from the hardware store of his truck to *hold*
for now electrical and structural salvations he believes

in the temporal the neighborly the seasonal the salvaging
of all re-usable metal and wood in the evitable

breakdowns coming towards us about which he chuckles
installs a stop valve and tightens the joint by hand

knowing a system undergoing a thermodynamic process
can never completely return to its previous state

and a leaky valve in faucet or heart requires mechanical
gods who say wiping their hands *it'll hold for now*

sutured duct-taped now rubber-banded now
stretching elastic now to reach at least next week

NOTES

"Alex, an Obituary": Animal psychologist Irene Pepperberg conducted a thirty-year experiment with Alex (1976–2007), an African grey parrot, as her research partner. Their work focused on reasoning skills and language acquisition.

"Scottish Melodies": Many regard William Marshall (1748–1833) as the greatest composer of Scottish fiddle tunes. Fiddlecase Books, founded in 1973 by Randy Miller and Jack Perron, currently publishes *William Marshall's Scottish Melodies*.

"Taken into Account": Italicized lines come from "'Sea Slaves': The Human Misery That Feeds Pets and Livestock," *New York Times*, July 27, 2015.

ACKNOWLEDGMENTS

I thank the editors of the following publications where these poems, some-times in different forms, originally appeared:

Academy of American Poets (poems.org): "The Barcelona Inside Me,"
"Men as Friends," "Hummingbird"; Alaska Quarterly Review: "Scottish
Melodies"; American Poetry Review: "The Collection of the Canter,"
"Elegy for the Science Teacher," "Hearing the News," "Missing,"
"Reading Music," "Rodeo Ben," "The Fix"; Bosque: "The Wages of
Sin," "Where the Unfairness of the World Resides"; Broadsided Press:
"Semblance"; Connotation Press: An Online Artifact: "Bluefish, 1970,"
"On the Grand Canal" "Taken Into Account"; Fourth River: "Alex,
an Obituary," "True Blue Communications Man"; Lavender Review:
"The Black Bear Inside Me"; The New Yorker: "Theory"; Ocean State
Review: "Coppice and Pollard," "A Moment of Amazement," "White-
tail Spring"; Poet Lore: "Security Clearance," "Ballroom"; Poetry Daily
(poems.com): "The Fix"; River Styx: "Provisional Ode;"

I appreciate the friends and readers who made this a better book, includ-
ing Julie Abraham, James Brasfield, John Daniels, Jan Freeman, Charlotte
Holmes, Susanna Kaysen, Amy Lang, Leslie Lawrence, Khyber and Maren
Oser, Carolyn Sachs, and Marianne Weil.